TV's Forgotten Hero

TV's Forgotten Hero

The Story of Philo Farnsworth

Stephanie Sammartino McPherson

Carolrhoda Books, Inc./Minneapolis

*For my parents, Angelo and Marion Sammartino,
who both appeared in early television shows.*

Carolrhoda Books, Inc. c/o The Lerner Group
241 First Avenue North, Minneapolis, MN 55401

Library of Congress Cataloging-in-Publication Data

McPherson, Stephanie Sammartino.
   TV's forgotten hero : the story of Philo Farnsworth / Stephanie
Sammartino McPherson.
      p.   cm.
   Includes bibliographical references and index.
   Summary: A biography of the persistent experimenter whose interest in
electricity led him to develop an electronic television system in the 1920s.
   ISBN 1-57505-017-X (lib. bdg.)
   1. Farnsworth, Philo Taylor, 1906–1971—Juvenile literature.
2. Inventors—United States—Biography—Juvenile literature.
3. Television—History—Juvenile literature. [1. Farnsworth, Philo
Taylor, 1906–1971. 2. Television—History.] I. Title.
TK6635.F3M37 1996
388'0092—dc20
[B]   95-26383

Manufactured in the United States of America
1 2 3 4 5 6 – JR – 01 00 99 98 97 96

Contents

During Philo Farnsworth's lifetime, television grew to play an important role in the way Americans live.

Introduction

All over the world people gazed, spellbound, at their television sets. A figure in a bulky suit filled the screen. Breathless, viewers watched the man step across a white, alien landscape. It was July 20, 1969, and the first astronauts had just landed on the moon.

Philo Farnsworth, a frail, careworn man of sixty-two, forgot everything else as he watched the scene. "This has made it all worthwhile," he told his wife, Pem.

Although Farnsworth was not connected with the Apollo moon landing, he felt responsible for the millions of people watching the event. Forty-two years earlier he had made the first all-electronic television transmission. Even then he had been dreaming about space travel, but he'd never imagined that a version of his television camera would journey to the moon.

By the beginning of the space age, most people took TV broadcasting for granted. They'd forgotten the many years Farnsworth and other inventors had worked to perfect television. Modern giant screen, color sets have come a long way from Farnsworth's first four-inch, black-and-white receiver. But without his basic inventions, television as we know it simply wouldn't exist.

Electricity At Last!

Wide-eyed, young Philo Farnsworth pored over the dog-eared pages of his favorite book. It was the Sears catalog, and to a boy from rural Utah in the early 1900s, it was full of wonders. To Philo, the alarm clocks, flashlights, and telegraph sets on the pages were small miracles.

Philo had never seen most of the things pictured in the catalog. The house where he lived with his parents and younger sisters and brother was a small, log structure with few modern conveniences. It certainly wasn't wired for electricity. Maybe that's why electricity seemed so mysterious and wonderful to Philo. By far the most exciting items in the catalog were the electric toy trains and the small electric motors. Over and over, Philo studied the pictures until he came up with a plan. Even though his family couldn't afford a motor or a train, he would make his own electricity.

In Philo Farnsworth's hometown, Beaver, Utah, many people living downtown had electricity. The Farnsworths didn't.

Philo took a walk around the farm. He was a thin boy with sandy hair, eager blue eyes, and a big imagination. Usually he looked for prairie dogs and lizards when he had time to go exploring. This time he stayed inside the farmyard to find spare buckets and boards, broken spokes, and small garden tools. Somehow from this heap of odds and ends, he meant to build a machine to make electricity.

Rolling up his sleeves, Philo began fitting the pieces together first one way, then the other. Finally he connected everything into a strange-looking device with lots of moving parts. It made quite a racket, but Philo's machine didn't light lamps or send toy trains circling around a track. Philo couldn't turn the physical energy of the moving parts into electrical energy. Still, the machine had been fun to make, and it was a sort of invention.

Philo had been thinking about inventions ever since he saw his first telephone and first gramophone. Although both devices had been around since the late 1800s, most of the families the Farnsworths knew didn't have either one. Six-year-old Philo had been thrilled to talk to his aunt Mary on the telephone. He had been delighted to turn the handle of the gramophone and hear music come out of the trumpet-shaped funnel on top. But when it stopped playing, he was full of questions. How did the music get into the gramophone? What made Aunt Mary's voice come out of the telephone? His eyes sparkled with excitement when he talked to his parents later. He was going to be an inventor when he grew up, he told them.

Lewis and Serena Farnsworth weren't going to stand in Philo's way. They believed that with dedication and hard work, a person could do anything. Together, Philo and his dad tackled several science projects. Philo especially liked building a framework out of bamboo poles and string. With this simple contraption, he could trace the movements of the stars and planets. Night after night, he studied the sky. Soon he could locate the planets and point out the constellations.

Philo's older half brothers and sisters from his father's first marriage also encouraged him. They read him stories about famous inventors such as Alexander Graham Bell and Thomas Edison. Philo just couldn't get enough of their stories. When he told the same stories to his younger sisters and brother, he made them so fascinating that Agnes, Laura, and Carl couldn't get enough of them either.

The Farnsworths were a close-knit Mormon family.

Lewis Farnsworth, Philo's father, was always looking for a better farm or for better opportunities for himself and his family.

They had little money and few belongings. In fact, they didn't even have a permanent home. Philo had been born August 19, 1906, in a log cabin near Beaver, Utah, but the family had moved when he was only four years old. Lewis Farnsworth was always looking for a better farm to support his growing family. Philo didn't mind changing houses and schools as long as they were all together. Then Mr. Farnsworth accepted a job that took him away from home. That was hard. When Philo's father left to clear land on an Indian reservation, the rest of the family moved into an isolated log cabin.

Philo's half brothers and sisters were grown by then. His mother, Serena, was left with four small children and a baby on the way. So Mr. Farnsworth asked eight-year-old Philo to be the "man of the family" for a while. As the "man," Philo led the cow to pasture, fed the pigs and chickens, and carried in the wood. His favorite job was taking care of Tippy, his very own pony. Philo had never had a pony before. He brushed Tippy's coat until it shone and led her to the greenest fields to graze. With so many chores, Philo didn't have much time for science. But his imagination was always on the go, thinking of the things he might invent someday.

After Philo's youngest brother, Lincoln, was born, his father decided to move the family to Vernal, Utah. Philo had to say good-bye to Tippy because his parents said the city was no place for a horse. Now, instead of riding, Philo got around by roller-skating. But he missed his pony, and even in the city, his house didn't have electricity. When the family packed up again to move to the small town of Washington in southern Utah, Philo wasn't sorry.

Once more Philo would have to change schools, but now he would live close to his grandparents. He would also be in a farm area where he could have animals. Philo gathered a flock of orphan lambs and decided to go into business raising them. The small, cuddly animals bleated constantly to be fed, but Philo had Agnes and Carl to help him. They held the lambs like babies and fed them milk from bottles.

When the lambs were big enough to sell, Philo knew just what he wanted to do with the money. He sat down with his grandma's Sears catalog and flipped through the pages. Finally he could order something from the book! The toy trains still looked good, but the bicycles looked even better. If only he could decide which one to order.

Hard as it was, Philo finally made a decision and showed it to his grandma. She admired the bicycle too.

Vernal, Utah, where the Farnsworths moved in the early 1900s, was bigger than any town where the family had previously lived.

But then she turned to a different part of the catalog. Philo stared. Why was she showing him the violins? With a sinking heart, he listened to his grandma describe the wonderful music he would be able to play on the violin.

Philo still wanted a bicycle, but he hated to disappoint his grandma. That night he dreamed about the violin. When he woke up, he was very excited. Yes, he would buy a violin, he decided. He would become a famous violinist, and people would come from all over the country to hear him play.

After his package arrived in the mail, Philo practiced constantly. Luckily, his grandma let him practice at her house so his baby brother didn't have to hear his wrong notes or the shrill squeaks of his bow over the violin strings. Over the next few months, the racket changed to simple songs that Philo's family could recognize. After a while, the Farnsworths even began to enjoy the music.

Philo was determined to be a great musician. Once he

even knocked down a boy for making fun of his violin. When the time came for the Farnsworths to move again, Philo packed his violin carefully.

Now the family was leaving Utah entirely. They were going to settle on a ranch in Idaho, and they were going to travel by covered wagon. In 1917 many people traveled by car or train. But Philo's family didn't own a car, and they couldn't take all their belongings on a train. Covered wagon seemed the best and cheapest way to go. Eleven-year-old Philo drove the third and last wagon in the family's caravan. He waved to his brothers and sisters in the back of the second wagon and watched the landscape roll by. He listened to the squawking hens and squealing piglets in his own wagon. Sometimes the trip was slow and boring, but visiting friends and relatives along the way was fun.

One day the wagons rolled off the trail and onto the paved streets of Salt Lake City. Large buildings rose on either side of Philo. Some of them had electricity, he thought, as he turned his eager gaze in every direction. Salt Lake City was the biggest town he had ever been to. And the Mormon Temple was the biggest building he had ever seen. So much had been accomplished since the first Mormon pioneers had come to Utah. Philo's own grandparents had helped establish some of the early Mormon settlements. Feeling a little like a pioneer himself, Philo straightened his shoulders and urged the horses forward.

Even when the Farnsworths arrived in Idaho, their travels weren't over. For a while they stayed in the town of Thomas. Then they moved several miles north to Ucon.

On their way to a new home in 1917, Philo and his family took their covered wagons through bustling Salt Lake City.

By the spring of 1919, the Farnsworths were packing up the covered wagons again. They were going to live with Philo's uncle Albert and his family on his ranch near Rigby, Idaho. Philo and his family drove their wagons to the borders of the 240-acre ranch. Approaching the granaries and two white houses, Philo saw something that made him catch his breath. All the buildings were connected by wires. Slowly a grin spread over his face. Those wires could mean only one thing.

Electricity at last!

Philo Farnsworth was already sure he wanted to be an inventor when this photograph was taken of him at age 13.

Always Tinkering

It didn't take Philo long to find the generator that powered his uncle's ranch. It was located in a small shed near the farmhouse, and Philo slipped inside as often as he could. Now he had a real machine to make electricity. When the generator was turned on, it sent power flowing along wires to light electric lamps in the house. It also pumped water through the pipes and heated the water in the hot water tank.

The farmhouse was much grander than anywhere else Philo had lived. For the first time in his life, he could take warm baths without having to heat the water on the stove. He could also read at night without straining his eyes. When Philo climbed up to the attic, he found piles of old science magazines. He probably would have read them all night, if his mother hadn't stopped him.

But Serena Farnsworth knew Philo had to get up early for his before-school job. Every morning Philo drove a large wagon to nearby farms to pick up children for school. In winter he drove a sleigh and left the house while it was still dark. His passengers brought hot bricks from the fireplace to keep warm in the subfreezing weather.

Between his job, school, and farm chores, Philo had plenty to do. But he still made time to experiment with electricity. He was bursting with questions. How much electricity could the generator produce at once? What would happen if he switched around the 32 one-volt batteries or plugged more lights into the sockets? Sometimes he tinkered too much. Then a fuse would blow, and all the lights on the farm would go out. Alone in the dark, Philo wondered how he could have prevented the mishap. But soon he was planning his next experiment. Meanwhile, his mother had to call the repairman, William Tall, again. Some weeks Mr. Tall had to drive his buggy out to the farm two or three times.

Although this was a bother for the repairman, it was fascinating for Philo. Every trip he learned a little more about the generator. He also made friends with Mr. Tall's twin sons, Asael and Aldon, who sometimes came along. Asael and Aldon were in Philo's Boy Scout troop and his grade at school. There was nothing the three boys liked better than to clown around and play jokes on each other. When the teacher read Mark Twain's *Huckleberry Finn* to the class, no one enjoyed the funny parts more than Philo. In fact, the twins were almost more amused by Philo's uproarious laughter than by the story itself.

Philo *(center)*, Vern Sorenson *(left)*, and another Rigby friend clown around.

No matter how busy he was with school and friends, Philo continued to tinker with the generator. And it continued to break down—even when he left it alone. One day Philo decided to fix it himself. While his father, uncle, and grown-up cousins watched, Philo took the machine apart and used kerosene to wipe away the heavy oil that had collected on its moving parts. Carefully he put the pieces together again. The generator worked! Philo had become "Farnsworth Farm's Chief Engineer."

The "Chief Engineer" was always trying something. He found an old motor in the shed and hooked it up to his mother's washing machine. Instead of pushing the handle on the washing machine back and forth, a chore Philo hated, he could simply turn on the electricity to set the clothes churning in the tub. That project was so much fun that Philo connected his mother's sewing machine to the motor too. Then he thought about how dark it was in the barn after sunset. Soon he was busy wiring the barn and hanging up electric lights. At the local bishop's request, he even wired the Mormon meetinghouse for electricity.

But Philo wanted to engineer much bigger things than home appliances and meetinghouses. With the money he earned driving the school wagon, he bought the latest copies of science magazines. He read every science book he could find and spent hours in the small lab he set up in the attic. It wasn't very fancy, but it was all Philo's own, a special place where he could be alone with his books and his ideas.

One day Philo found an article about an exciting idea called television. In 1919 most people still hadn't had a chance to experience radio. It would be a year before the first commercial radio stations began to broadcast, and then they would only reach a small percentage of the population. But the idea of television had been around for a long time. Even Alexander Graham Bell had dreamed of transmitting pictures as well as voices over long distances.

Some inventors had already tried to make this dream a reality. As early as 1884, a German scientist named Paul Nipkow invented a round, mechanical disk with a series of tiny holes. Light reflected by an object flickered through these holes and was changed into electricity. The electricity contained a picture of the object in a special coded form. Brighter parts of the object generated more electricity than the darker parts.

When the electricity reached its destination, it passed through an identical disk, spinning at the same rate as the first one. The second disk decoded the electrical signals, and the picture appeared on a receiving station. Although he owned a patent, Nipkow had never tested his device. However, in the early 1900s other scientists were beginning to investigate his ideas.

Once Philo read his first story about television, he could scarcely think of anything else. He imagined pictures of faraway places appearing right in his own house.

Even before television was invented, people speculated about its uses. This cartoon shows a woman taking a televised class at home.

This was more than just an incredible toy, he told his brothers and sisters. This was a real-life science adventure, something that could change the world as much as the telephone or electric lights.

German scientist Paul Nipkow theorized that spinning disks could be used to send images. Although Nipkow never put his ideas into practice, others experimented with Nipkow disks in the early 1900s.

First, of course, there were problems to solve. Could Nipkow's spinning disk produce a really clear picture? As fascinated as he was by the idea of television, Philo didn't think so. "Nothing mechanical can move fast enough," he said. A picture produced by a spinning mechanical disk would be blurry, and there was always the chance the moving parts would break down.

Still, there had to be a way to make television work. Philo believed he could find it if he just studied hard enough. He continued to read books and magazines, but more of the articles were about automobiles than television. Automobiles weren't just a dream. In large cities, they had begun to replace horses. When Philo read about a national contest to see who could create the best invention to improve the automobile, he was thrilled. The winner would receive a twenty-five-dollar prize. What a lot of science books that would buy!

Philo rarely rode in the new Model T Fords and other horseless carriages. But he did have an idea to improve them. He decided to invent an ignition lock that would keep automobiles from being stolen. The ignition is where the driver inserts the key to start the engine. Philo's readings in electronics convinced him that he could magnetize certain parts of the ignition lock. Then only a specially magnetized key would start the car. Without that key, no one could steal the car.

Philo was thinking about how to magnetize the key one day as he held the reins to a three-horse team and guided the plow across a field. He didn't notice when one of the reins slipped from his grasp and began to drag on the ground. But his father noticed and knew how dangerous it was. If something startled the horse, it might start running and throw Philo against the sharp points of the plow. Scarcely daring to breathe, Lewis Farnsworth walked across the field and took the fallen rein. Philo realized the danger he'd been in and suddenly felt weak in the knees, but he still couldn't stop thinking about the contest. "Papa, Papa! I've got it!" he cried. "This idea will win the prize!"

The next day Philo's older cousin Kent took him to see a man who had been in an accident and wrecked his car. Since there was no way to fix the car, the man gave Philo the ignition and the two keys that fit it. Gratefully Philo lugged it all home. He spent every spare moment working on his invention. When the burglarproof lock was completed, a reporter came out from the Rigby newspaper to interview Philo. He became a hero before he even entered the contest.

Philo was right about how good his idea was. That fall he received the twenty-five-dollar award for first place. Although he'd planned to buy science books, he decided he needed a grown-up suit with long pants even more. Philo had joined a small orchestra that played for dances, and he didn't want the audience to see him in his knickers.

Each week Philo earned five dollars playing in the orchestra, and he did use that money for books. He also kept experimenting. One day he attached a wire to a telephone pole and strung it all the way to his friend Vernal Sorenson's house. Carefully he fastened a wire to another telephone line and strung it to his own house. He could hardly wait to try sending Vern messages in Morse code.

But the nearby farmers couldn't wait to find out why their telephones weren't working. Soon they discovered the extra wires on the phone lines. No one was really surprised to learn that Philo was responsible. He might not be an inventor yet, but already Philo Farnsworth had a reputation for always tinkering.

Philo's Great Idea

Philo still daydreamed sometimes when he plowed, but he tried to remember to stop working when he had important things to think over. One day he halted the horses at the end of a row and turned to look back over the field. The long furrows of dirt were as straight and even as a line of print—perfect for planting beets. And maybe perfect for something else too, Philo realized, remembering the articles he'd read about television.

The field lay behind him like a great picture made of lines. What if, instead of beets, each line contained small pieces of a large picture such as a house or person? One line by itself wouldn't mean much, but together they would make a complete image. Here was a new way to transmit television, Philo thought—line by line. Each line could be converted into electricity and sent over a distance. At the receiving end, the electrical units could be reassembled into the same pattern and turned back into a picture. No one would even see the individual lines assembling on the screen. Everything would happen so quickly that the viewer would see only the completed picture.

Up and down the beet field, Philo continued to guide his horses, but his mind was far away. He had read several articles about electrons, tiny charged particles whose paths could be bent to form an electrical circuit. Maybe they were the key to television. Philo's heart beat quickly. He wanted to jump up and down, run across the field, and shout his discovery out loud. Instead, he kept the horses to their steady pace across the field, dividing it into lines, just as he hoped someday to divide and reassemble a picture.

Later that afternoon, Philo shared his news with his father. Lewis Farnsworth couldn't begin to understand everything Philo was talking about, but he listened carefully. Maybe this *was* the answer to television. Philo seemed so certain of it. "It's all right, son, to have your head in the clouds," Lewis said, "so long as you keep your feet firmly planted on the ground."

Philo determined to keep his feet on the ground by studying even harder. If only he knew enough, he might find a way to make his idea work. After a long day of schoolwork and farm jobs, he spent his evenings reading and planning.

When fifteen-year-old Philo started high school that fall, he was far ahead of his classmates in science. Although he was only a freshman, he convinced chemistry teacher Justin Tolman to let him join the senior chemistry class. Soon Mr. Tolman wondered what he'd gotten himself into. He spent hours answering Philo's many questions and helping him catch up on the work he'd missed.

Rigby High School

Some days Philo had a dozen questions for his surprised teacher. And he didn't limit them to the classroom. Wherever he met Mr. Tolman—at school or in town—Philo usually had something on his mind.

Although Mr. Tolman couldn't answer all of Philo's questions, he encouraged his star student to be an inventor. He even loaned Philo books from his personal library. Philo was especially fascinated by one book on cathode-ray tubes, glass tubes from which all the air is removed. Inside a cathode-ray tube, Philo learned, there was nothing to interfere with the movement of electrons.

Early radios had no speakers. Listeners had to wear headphones when they tuned in their favorite shows.

This meant the electrons could be arranged to form different patterns. Philo read the book over and over again. By the time he returned the book to his teacher, it was practically falling apart.

Whatever he did, a little part of Philo was always thinking about television. Most people were still getting used to the radio. Philo's family didn't have a radio, but some of his wealthier friends did. Philo loved to go to their radio parties. Only one person at a time could listen since early radios had no speakers, only earphones. "Someday you'll look at the tube and see the performers," Philo told his friends. Asael and Aldon and Vern laughed at what sounded like a joke, but deep down, they had to wonder—was Philo right?

Philo didn't really expect his friends to understand, but he did want to discuss his ideas with someone. One day after school, he hurried to the empty chemistry classroom. He picked up a piece of chalk and began to draw diagrams all over the blackboard. When Mr. Tolman entered the room, Philo's heartbeat quickened. "What is that?" demanded the teacher.

"It's an electrical system for projecting an image," Philo answered. He managed to keep his voice calm, but inside Philo was nervous. He felt a great deal depended on this meeting.

Mr. Tolman shook his head in confusion. "But what does that have to do with our chemistry assignment?"

"Oh nothing," Philo admitted. "It's my new invention." Then he picked up a pointer and launched into a careful explanation.

Justin Tolman was impressed by Philo Farnsworth's ability to grasp complex subjects. Once when Tolman passed by a study hall, he was astonished to realize that Philo was explaining Einstein's theory of relativity to his classmates.

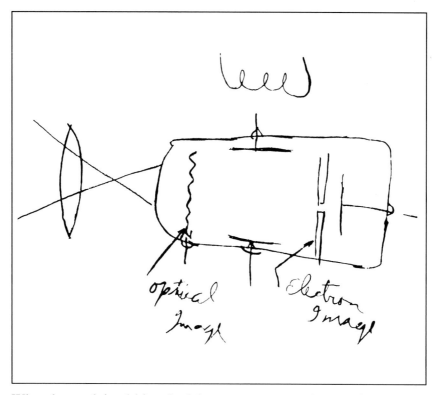

When he explained his television system to teacher Justin Tolman, Philo sketched this diagram of the image dissector, an electronic television camera.

There were two major parts to his system, Philo said, the image dissector (television camera) and the cathode-ray tube (television receiver). Inside the image dissector, the picture (image) would be divided up (dissected) into lines and changed into electricity. In the cathode-ray tube, electricity would be changed back into pictures.

By this time, fifteen-year-old Philo had already decided how he could do all this. He couldn't wait to explain the technical details to Mr. Tolman. What would his teacher say?

At first, it was all Mr. Tolman could do just to keep up with Philo's reasoning and mathematics. The next day after school and several more times after that, he sat down with Philo to talk about the television system. Slowly it began to make sense to the startled teacher. Philo's idea seemed fantastic. But, as Tolman told the relieved and happy inventor, it just might work.

People often remarked that Philo looked older than his age, he had so much on his mind. In this photograph, Philo was just 17.

Finding Time for Television

More than anything, Philo wanted to build his television system and try it out. But that would take much more money than the Farnsworths had and more time than Philo could spare. Besides being an inventor, Philo was still a farmer's son. That spring he left school to help his father with the planting on yet another farm. The Farnsworths were struggling financially, and they needed a good harvest if they were going to make a go of it. All through the summer, Philo worked on the farm and studied electronics through a mail-order course offered by the National Radio Institute.

By the end of the summer, Philo's father still wasn't making enough on the farm to pay all the bills. He decided to move again, this time to Provo, Utah. Philo had just earned his electrician's license from the radio institute. Although he was only sixteen, he decided it was time he got a job.

Instead of going to Provo, Philo moved to Glenns Ferry, Idaho, where his half brother Lew had a railroad job. Philo became an electrician for the Oregon Short Line Railroad. When the trains were changing tracks at the station, Philo had to make sure the headlights were focusing correctly. Nervously he climbed on the engine as it slowly swung around on the turnstile. Philo didn't like working on the outside of a moving train—especially when it rained or snowed. One false move, and he could easily wind up on the tracks. But at least he was making money. He used his wages to take several correspondence courses from the University of Utah.

One year later, in the fall of 1923, Philo joined his parents in Provo. Although he hadn't graduated from high school in Idaho, he managed to enroll in Brigham Young University as a special student working to finish his high school diploma. He studied hard and even helped his older cousin with a college physics course.

In the middle of all this activity, Philo's father became ill. In January 1924, Lewis Farnsworth died of pneumonia. Philo was beside himself with grief, but he knew he had to be strong for his mother. Now, more than ever, his family depended on him. As the oldest child of his father's second family, Philo felt a tremendous responsibility to support his brothers and sisters. When the school year was over, he decided to join the United States Navy. As a navy man, he could send money home and perhaps study at the naval academy in Annapolis, Maryland.

First, however, Philo had to go to boot camp in San Diego, California. Even though he earned the second highest score in the nation on his entrance exam, he soon knew that navy life was not for him. He didn't like the fancy dress drills or the guard duty at the military prison. He especially didn't like being nicknamed Fido by the other recruits. From then on he told everyone to call him just plain Phil.

With the help of a navy chaplain, Phil Farnsworth got an early release from military service. Still determined to help his mother, he returned to Provo and enrolled again at Brigham Young University. Phil got a student loan, a part-time job, and settled in to learn all he could about electronics.

One day Phil came home and found his sister Agnes had invited a friend over for lunch. Immediately he liked Elma Gardner, nicknamed Pem. She was pretty and friendly—someone Phil found easy to talk to. But Pem was still in high school, and Phil didn't run into her again for quite a while. He kept busy with classes, rehearsals for the college orchestra, and a job installing radios and antennas for a furniture store.

Time passed quickly with so much to do. But Phil hadn't forgotten how to have fun. After several months of hard work, he decided to celebrate with a radio party. First, he wrote to some distant radio stations. Then he borrowed one of the best radios from the store where he worked and invited all his friends and Agnes's friend Pem. Everyone was delighted when radio announcers in Los Angeles and Cincinnati mentioned Phil Farnsworth by name and played several songs just for him. But the most impressed of all was Pem Gardner.

When Phil learned that Pem and her brother Cliff were musicians, he decided to form a small group. Pem played the piano, Cliff played the trombone, and Phil played the violin. The more Phil got to know Pem, the more he felt himself drawn to her. That spring the Gardner family moved into the empty half of a duplex where the Farnsworths already lived. For a while Phil and Pem saw each other often. But as soon as the school year ended, Phil left for Payson Canyon, Utah, where he had a summer job with a lumber company.

In the fall of 1925, Phil looked desperately for another job in Provo to support him through the school year at Brigham Young University. The economy was so bad that he had to go all the way to Salt Lake City to find work. Phil wouldn't be able to attend the university after all.

Every weekend, however, Phil returned home to Provo. He took Pem to dances and church socials. After one date, they danced all the way home. Phil wanted to share his serious side with Pem too. One day he took her horseback riding through Provo Canyon to a noisy and beautiful waterfall named Bridal Veil. For the first time, he told Pem about television and how he planned to make it work. Excitedly he explained that he had already figured out a way to send pictures along with radio waves. He simply needed a chance to put his plan into action.

Pem listened in amazement. Here was a side to Phil she hadn't suspected at all. But she never doubted for a moment he could do what he said. Pem told Phil that his idea sounded wonderful, and she hoped he had a chance to build his invention soon.

When Phil met Pem Gardner, he hoped she would share his interest in television. A woman he dated earlier dropped him when he told her of his invention. She wanted to be with a man who was "going somewhere," she said.

These were just the words Phil hoped to hear! Already he knew he wanted Pem by his side when he got the chance to work on television.

Meanwhile other people were thinking about television too. Phil knew this from the science magazines he continued to read. Although the other experimenters used mechanical disks, it seemed just a matter of time until somebody else thought of Phil's electronic approach. But he had no money for equipment to test his ideas. He barely earned enough to make ends meet and to help his family.

Finally Phil found a position with the Salt Lake City Community Chest, an organization which raised money for local charities. Phil supervised a staff of six students and soon needed even more help. He knew that Pem and Cliff would be good at the job, but he had a personal reason for suggesting them to his bosses. Recently Phil and Pem had become engaged. After she joined the small staff, Phil would see her every day.

Phil's bosses, George Everson and Leslie Gorrell, liked the eager, earnest young man. Often it was hard for them to realize that Phil was only nineteen. He looked older and seemed to have something on his mind. One night, when Everson and Gorrell asked about his future plans, Phil said he had an idea for an invention, but he'd probably never get the funds to do something about it.

The two men studied Phil curiously. "What is your idea?" asked Gorrell.

"It's a television system," said Phil.

"Television system!" Now the men were frankly staring. They weren't even sure what a television system was, but they were amazed at how seriously Phil talked about it. On the outside, Phil seemed shy and preoccupied. Now his bosses recognized that on the inside he was an incredible dreamer. That's all television seemed to them at first—a fantastic dream. Later that evening, however, Everson and Gorrell began to wonder if it really was just a dream. Phil had made some very good points. Maybe they should learn more about his invention.

The next night Everson and Gorrell took Phil out to dinner. When Phil explained the details of his electronic television system, he seemed like a different person. His eyes shone, and he spoke with deep feeling and confidence. The two older men began to catch some of his excitement.

Phil talked about what other scientists were doing. In England John Logie Baird had already transmitted rough pictures. In the United States, Charles Francis Jenkins, hard at work on what he called "Radio Vision," had broadcast moving pictures of a windmill. "They are all barking up the wrong tree," Phil told his bosses. He was convinced that the mechanical disks these men used would never be practical. They could never scan an image fast enough to provide a clear picture. Phil explained that his own system had no moving parts. Carefully controlled electrons in the image dissector and the cathode-ray tube did all the work, and they did it at a speed mechanical parts could never match.

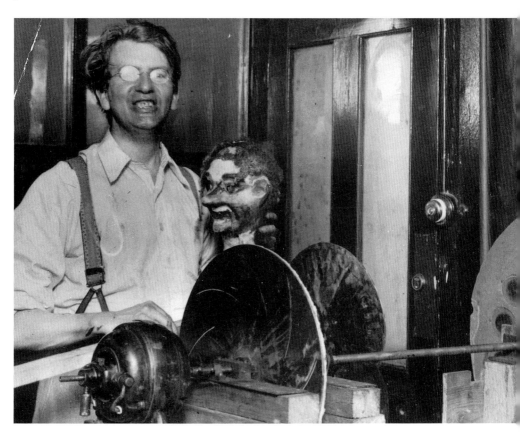

In England in the 1920s, John Logie Baird used a version of Nipkow's disks to televise images. Beneath the camera's bright, hot lights, people would faint, so Baird televised the head of a ventriloquist's dummy.

Les Gorrell, Phil Farnsworth, and George Everson

When their fund-raising campaign came to a halt, Everson and Gorrell decided to go into partnership with the ambitious young man. They would use their own money to finance his invention.

As soon as he heard the news, an excited Phil called up Pem. "Can you be ready to be married in three days?" he asked. Quickly he explained what had happened. Then he said he wanted to move to California. The state had some of the best libraries and labs in the country, and Phil wanted to be able to use them. But he wouldn't move without Pem.

Pem declared she couldn't possibly be ready. But three hectic days later on May 27, 1926, nineteen-year-old Phil and eighteen-year-old Pem were married at her father's home in Provo. "There is another woman in my life," Phil told his bride that night, "and her name is Television." Pem hadn't thought of it that way before. Life with an inventor promised to be full of surprises.

The day after their wedding, Phil and Pem took the train to Los Angeles. They found an inexpensive, four-room apartment in Hollywood and began turning the dining room into a lab. But even before he bought the lenses and wires and other supplies he needed, Phil rented a piano. After a long day working on television, he was going to need a little music.

Over the next few months, Pem would sit at the keyboard while Phil played his violin. Sometimes Phil liked to make up tunes at the piano too. Concentrating on the music, Phil would feel the pressure of his work ebb away, but not the excitement. It was as if a part of his brain was working on television at the same time he was relaxing with the music.

Just finding the radio tubes and other supplies he needed taxed Phil's imagination. When George Everson and Les Gorrell arrived in June to see how he was doing, Phil still hadn't found the specially shaped vacuum tube he needed for his image dissector. The three men spent several days driving to stores all over Los Angeles. Although they bought a good bit of equipment, the kind of tube Phil was looking for simply didn't exist. At last he found a glassblower willing to make it for him.

The finished tube had a large flat end coated inside with a special light-sensitive substance. This was Phil's earliest version of an image dissector, or television camera. The picture to be televised would be focused onto the light-sensitive surface. As the light from the picture struck this surface, electrons would be given off. Where light from a bright part of the picture hit the surface, many electrons would come off. Where light from a darker part of the picture hit the surface, fewer electrons would break free.

Phil had to collect these electrons, line by line, in order to transmit them to a television set. From his readings, he knew that magnets could be used to direct the flow of electrons. He figured he could wrap magnetic coils around the image dissector tube and use them to control the electrons. The coils would tug at the electrons, pulling them, line by line, in front of an opening or electronic eye. In a single long stream, the electrons would pass into the opening.

Now the picture could be transmitted as electricity to another location. At the receiving end, the cathode-ray tube would act as a television set. It would amplify the electricity until a strong current had been built up. The current would pass into the back of the television set, and electrons would be given off. Then these electrons would be directed, line by line, to the larger front part of the set. Here the television set had been coated with phosphor, a substance which is sensitive to electrons. As electrons hit the surface, they would give off light, and a picture would appear on the screen.

Phil knew his system would work, but putting it together was a tremendous challenge. Throughout the summer, his friends and backers, George and Les, came to visit him. Often they carried strange-looking equipment.

Image Dissector Tube
(Television Camera)

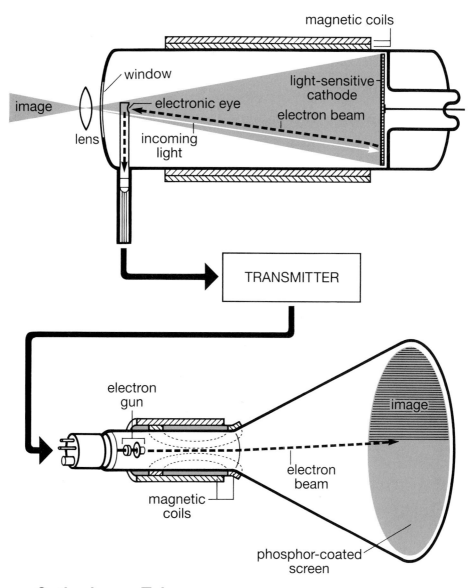

Cathode-ray Tube
(Television Receiver)

Sometimes they worked too. George wound yards of coils in the backyard. The coils would be used to guide the electrons given off in the image dissector. Other coils would direct the pattern the electrons made in the television set.

A motor droning noisily in the garage provided the electrical power Phil needed for his experiments. The neighbors wondered what it was doing there. When their radio reception became fuzzy, they decided to investigate the odd tenants in Apartment 1339.

Phil didn't worry much about what the neighbors thought until the police showed up. The officers were checking out rumors of an illegal still used to make bootleg liquor! Phil and Pem were shocked and a little amused, but they stood aside while the police searched their apartment. "Well, I'll be darned," mumbled one of the officers when Phil explained it was his new television system.

After the police left, Phil and Pem probably shared a good laugh, but soon Phil was back at work again. He knew he was getting close to his goal. Maybe the next time a police officer knocked at his door, Phil could show off a real picture.

After many weeks of hard work, Phil was finally ready to test his system. Pem, George, and Les gathered in the dining room as Phil made a last-minute check of his equipment and turned on the motor. All eyes were on the cathode-ray tube where the electronic picture was supposed to appear. But nothing happened. Instead there was a noise like an exploding firecracker. Smoke began to fill the room. The electric current that flowed through the system had been too strong, and every single tube had blown out.

Horrified, Phil surveyed the scene. It was bad enough to fail, but it was even worse to fail in front of his backers. His very future seemed to be going up in smoke with his equipment.

Second Chance

Phil's partners weren't ready to give up on him. "Hey, it's not the end of the world!" said Les before the smoke had even cleared. Soon the partners were discussing what to do next. First, they decided Phil should write up his proposal to show to a patent attorney. The attorney could help him protect his ideas. If Phil's ideas were patented, other people couldn't use them to develop their own television systems. Phil, George, and Les would also get an evaluation of Phil's work from a top scientist. Once they had a scientific judgment, they could go to other investors for money. It looked like television was going to cost much more than the original six thousand dollars Phil had received.

Several days later a very nervous Phil showed up for his scheduled meeting with two lawyers and a scientist. But Phil couldn't stay nervous for long—not when he was talking about television. He was articulate, passionate, and thoroughly convincing. Finally one of the lawyers rose from his seat and cried, "This is a monstrous idea—a monstrous idea!"

Phil stared. He thought his idea was wonderful, not monstrous.

"The daring of this young man's intellect!" continued the lawyer. And suddenly Phil realized everything was fine after all. The lawyer was simply stunned by such an amazing idea.

Phil went on talking and answering questions for hours. Finally it was George's turn to ask some crucial questions. Were Phil's ideas scientifically correct? Were they original? Could they be made to work? The answer to all these questions was yes, just as Phil had known it would be.

When he worked at his lab—and even when he wasn't working—Phil's mind was full of new ideas and new ways to improve television.

Of course, there was still money and more hard work standing between Phil and his goal. He needed a new image dissector and other tubes and supplies. George might be a professional fund-raiser, but maybe he wouldn't find someone willing to trust a wild-sounding scheme like television. Weeks passed, and Phil grew fidgety and tense. Then good news came from George in San Francisco. He had found some people interested in learning more about television. Phil hurried to join his friend and soon had exactly what he wanted, a second chance. A group of bankers would invest twenty-five thousand dollars in his invention and give him one year to make his television system work. When Phil returned home and told Pem the news, they danced around the room. The very next day they moved to San Francisco.

Cliff Gardner, Pem's brother, was Phil's first paid lab assistant.

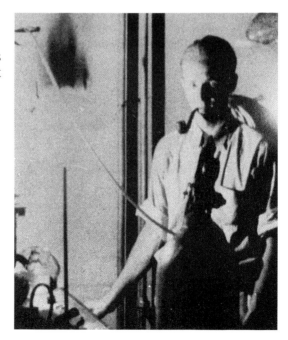

Before Phil and Pem even found a place to live, they went to see the work space Phil's new investors had given him on Green Street. It was just a loft over a garage, but as Phil strode into the big, empty space, his imagination was already filling it with equipment. He was full of plans to turn the loft into a real lab.

That evening Phil, Pem, and Pem's brother Cliff took the ferryboat across the bay into Oakland where they rented a small house. Every morning Phil and Cliff took the boat into San Francisco. Watching the distant buildings loom larger, Phil admired the skyline but wished he could get to his lab faster. Sometimes he didn't return home until late at night. Finally Pem got so tired of waiting for the men that she decided to work on television too. She did scientific drawings and record keeping and enjoyed the bustle of the lab as much as Phil did himself.

By that time, Phil already had a new image dissector tube hooked up to a vacuum system. The system pumped all the air out of the tube, so the air wouldn't affect the way electrons moved in the image dissector. The pumping took many hours. Then Phil had to vaporize light-sensitive potassium, turning the solid chemical into a gas. He also had to get the potassium to spread evenly on the far end of the tube. Meanwhile Cliff was learning glassblowing so he could make new tubes. It would take many tries and many tubes to make television practical.

Phil met each challenge with joyful determination. He could keep going hour after hour, day after day, because he loved what he was doing. While the details might be perplexing, he knew his general principles were sound.

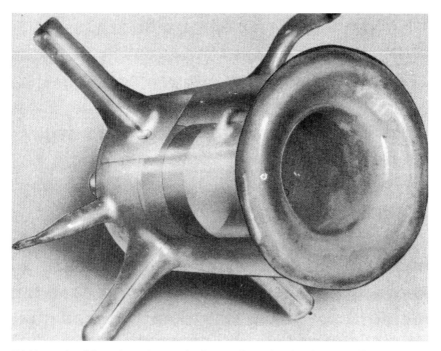

Phil made this tube, the main ingredient in the image dissector, in about 1926. According to Pem, it didn't work, but later attempts were more successful.

The whole secret was getting electrons to do what he wanted them to. "Control their speed," Phil said, "control their direction, change light—or pictures—into electricity and electricity into pictures at the other end of the telecast, and you'll have television."

Phil spent months trying to control electrons. He and Pem gave up their comfortable house in Oakland for a small city apartment so Phil could spend more time in the lab. Soon Phil's sister Agnes and Pem's sister Ruth came for extended visits with the young couple. Then an electronics engineer who was going to help in the lab moved in too. There wasn't much space left, but Phil and Pem didn't mind. They believed that families and friends were meant to stick together.

Even when he fell asleep at night, Phil often thought about his work. He'd set his alarm an hour early to give himself extra thinking time in the morning. Lying in bed, relaxing and concentrating at the same time, he often came up with the answer he was looking for. Then he'd hurry to the lab to test his newest solution.

No matter how hard he worked, Phil tried to keep his sense of humor. When his new financial backers or other visitors came to the lab, he liked to startle them by dropping potassium pellets into water, producing sudden, dramatic flames. Or he'd stick a piece of flexible hose into a chemical that froze it instantly. Phil would snap the rubber into pieces as easily as breaking a twig. These tricks had nothing to do with television, but Phil enjoyed the way visitors gasped and stared. After his performance, he'd talk some more about his real work.

Phil had made tremendous progress. He'd experimented with light-sensitive chemicals and learned to use magnetic coils for focusing. With Cliff's help, he'd turned making new dissector tubes into a routine science. Pem had learned to do welding so she could help make equipment too. And Phil was working on ways to amplify or strengthen signals in the receiver. But he hadn't transmitted a picture yet. It was the summer of 1927, and the year his backers had given him was running out. Phil could count on one hand the weeks he had left to make television work.

The Genius of Green Street

On September 7, 1927, Phil and his two new assistants gathered around the electronic receiver. It was time to test Phil's system again. The viewing screen, only four inches in diameter, was set into an oblong wooden box, and it glowed with a bluish light. This first electronic television set was connected by wire to an image dissector in a small room lined with copper. The copper prevented stray radio or electrical signals from interfering with the equipment. While the lab gang (as Phil sometimes called his staff) waited, Cliff slipped a glass slide with a line drawn across it in front of the image dissector. Immediately a horizontal, blurred line split the tiny screen of the receiver. Heart pounding, Phil made some changes with the focusing coils. The image sharpened into a thin, clear line.

Phil points proudly to the first successful television receiver, what he called the cathode-ray tube.

Phil yelled to Cliff to move the slide around. The viewers caught their breath as the line on the television screen began to shift positions too. Here was positive proof that the line they were seeing was the same line Cliff was transmitting from the next room. Phil's voice shook slightly as he announced, "That's it folks! We've done it! There you have electronic television!"

Even while George clapped him on the back and Pem jumped up and down, Phil was already thinking about what to do next. For this test, he had set up magnetic coils to scan from side to side, but not up and down. That's why he could only transmit a one-dimensional picture or straight line. The next step would be to send a two-dimensional picture over the wire. Satisfied that Phil was

on the right track, his backers agreed to continue support-
ing him.

Eight months later, the lab gang was clustered around
the receiver again. This time a blurred triangle appeared
on the screen. The simple shape meant that the up-and-
down scanning coils were working. Phil wanted a clearer
picture, so he began fussing with the controls on the television set. Instead of sharpening the image, Phil saw the
triangle disappear behind a moving pattern of spirals and
swirls that didn't look like anything at all. Alarmed, Phil
raced to the transmitter where Cliff was working. When
he saw his brother-in-law with a lit cigarette, Phil knew
exactly what had happened. The cigarette smoke had
been televised! Now Phil knew he would be able to transmit moving pictures. The lab gang went wild.

Phil knew it would take more than smoke to satisfy his
backers. The next day he planned a special demonstration
just for them. One of the backers, impatient for a profit,
had often asked when he was going to see some dollar
signs in Phil's invention. Phil gave him the answer by
televising a thick, black dollar sign.

The backers broke into appreciative laughter. Not only
was Phil smart, he had a good sense of humor. But delighted as they were with Phil's progress, they were getting restless. They wanted to make money as soon as
possible and thought the best way might be to sell their
shares in television to a large company that could complete the job Phil had begun.

This was the last thing in the world Phil wanted. But if
his backers withdrew their support, what would he do?

Once he had a working image dissector, Phil couldn't have been prouder of his experimental television camera.

Where would he get the money to finish his invention? In spite of his uncertain future, Phil worked harder than ever and added several members to his staff.

Day by day, television was improving. If only Phil could have been sure of his funding, he would have been perfectly happy. Finally the backers decided to hold a press conference. If the public knew more about electronic television, the backers might find a buyer for their investment.

Phil wasn't eager for a press conference. Although he'd applied for patents to protect his work, they hadn't been granted yet. Meanwhile John Logie Baird and Charles Francis Jenkins were still working with mechanical disks. Television experiments were also going on in large research labs run by the Bell and Westinghouse companies. Any of these researchers could explore Phil's approach after seeing the publicity. But despite the risk, on September 1, 1928, Phil opened up his lab to reporters.

The day after his press conference Phil went to a movie, then stopped to buy the *San Francisco Chronicle* from a newsboy. Beside him in the car, Pem flipped through the pages until she caught her breath at a headline: "S.F. Man's Invention to Revolutionize Television."

After the news conference in 1928 and the newspaper articles that followed it, Phil found that he had become a celebrity.

Next to the newspaper story was a picture of Phil, looking very much like the "young genius" the paper called him. He held an image dissector tube in one hand and a cathode-ray tube in the other. Phil listened to Pem read the story. It was a wonderful tribute, but it was also a little frightening. "This leaves us wide open to our competition," Phil said.

The story of Phil's triumph spread from newspaper to newspaper across the country and the world. His concept was simple enough to understand and fantastic enough to intrigue the public. Suddenly he wasn't an unknown inventor anymore. Phil was a public figure, someone scientists wanted to meet and someone large electronic companies couldn't afford to ignore. More visitors started dropping by the lab on Green Street. Phil was basically a shy person, but when he began explaining his work, he forgot everything else—even how famous and important some of his visitors were.

But Phil never forgot that the men who worked for him were important too. He encouraged them to think for themselves, test new solutions, and patent promising developments in their own names. "You worked *with* Phil, not *for* him," one of his colleagues said. "He never asked us to do anything he couldn't or wouldn't do."

To keep the lab running, Phil took jobs on the side improving the sound systems in several San Francisco theaters. In his free time, he played tennis with Pem, Cliff, and Cliff's wife, Lola. One Sunday in the middle of a game, a police officer appeared and announced that Phil's lab was on fire.

Dashing to the scene, Phil discovered that firefighters were having an almost impossible time. Whenever they sprayed water on the fire, something in the lab exploded. Quickly Phil explained that certain chemicals in the lab were reacting with the water. Then Phil told the firefighters what chemicals they could use to put out the flames. But it was too late to save the lab. Later when Phil climbed the stairs to the second floor loft, he found nothing but blackened walls and charred, useless equipment.

For a moment he stared in shocked silence, wondering where he would find money for repairs. But Phil knew that somehow he would find a way to continue his dream.

Aiming for Perfection

Luckily, Phil's backers had insured the lab, so he received money to rebuild it. One month later he was back at work and ready to try something new. First he bought an old movie projector and several film clips, including scenes from a hockey game, a prizefight, and the famous actress Mary Pickford in a Shakespearean play. Phil ran the films on the projector and televised the moving pictures. Day after day, Phil watched Mary Pickford combing her hair on television. At first only her face was in focus. The background and her clothing were too blurry to make out. As Phil worked on his electronic scanning system, the setting slowly took shape. Whenever George visited the lab, he found new details. Phil's first backer was thrilled at such rapid progress. By this time, Phil's televised pictures consisted of 100 to 150 lines. In one second, 30 separate pictures passed across the screen, but they appeared so quickly that they seemed like one.

Phil and his "lab gang" constantly worked to improve the television image, sometimes televising movie footage.

In 1929 Phil formed his own company, Television, Inc., with several other men. Now he didn't have to worry about his backers selling their interest in television to someone else. He also had the financial security to buy a row house in the city. Owning a home was important to Phil because Pem was expecting a baby. When Philo Taylor Jr. was born on September 23, 1929, the new home—with a nursery and a rocking chair—was all ready.

Each evening Phil held his new son, told Pem what happened in the lab, and then sometimes slipped away to work in his study. The third floor room had a doorway that led to the roof where Phil liked to watch airplanes on their way in and out of the city. He was almost as fascinated by flying as he was by television. At a time when most people considered an airplane trip a risky adventure, Phil was already thinking about space travel. Once he had even told Pem that he hoped to travel in space himself. "I think there are beings out there who have far surpassed us in development, mentally and otherwise," said Phil. "I intend to take an expedition out there someday and find them."

In the meantime, Phil continued to aim for perfection in the lab. Now he had two television systems—one with a four-inch screen and one with a seven-inch screen. Visitors flocked to his lab to see them work. Guglielmo Marconi, inventor of the telegraph, came to the Green Street lab, and so did Herbert Hoover Jr., the oldest son of the president of the United States. In April 1930, Vladimir Zworykin, another television pioneer, visited. Phil enjoyed talking with someone who shared his belief in the importance of electronics. He spent three days with the Russian immigrant and even let him watch Cliff make an image dissector tube. "This is a beautiful instrument," said Zworykin. "I wish that I might have invented it."

Russian-born inventor Vladimir Zworykin was Phil's main rival in the race to create a practical television system. Here Zworykin holds his iconoscope, an experimental camera tube.

As far as Farnsworth knew, Zworykin was his only real rival in electronic television. In 1923 Zworykin had applied for a patent on an electronic television system that operated differently from Phil's. The application had been denied because there were several parts that didn't work correctly, but Phil was certain Vladimir Zworykin would keep on trying—especially after this visit. That meant Phil had to redouble his own efforts.

On August 26, just one week after Phil's twenty-fourth birthday, he received the patents he'd been waiting for. Phil had beaten his competitors. No electronic television system had been patented before.

Elated by his victory, Phil wanted to put his invention to work. So far his broadcasts had been over electric wires. Late in 1930, Phil set up a radio transmitter on the roof of his lab. It was time for an experiment without any wires at all. Another television, placed in a building across town, would receive the transmission. The picture was fuzzy, but viewers could recognize it. For the first time, all-electronic pictures had been sent through the air.

Experimental broadcasts were one thing, but Phil believed that one day programs would be regularly scheduled just as radio shows were. Before this could happen, however, the government had to get involved. The Federal Radio Commission (later the Federal Communication Commission or FCC) regulated all broadcasts sent over radio waves. It assigned every radio station a single frequency at which it could transmit. This kept radio signals from getting mixed up with each other. It also meant that when listeners tuned in a station, the sound was clear.

The sharpness of Phil's television picture gradually improved, as this 1932 test (showing 3-year-old Philo Jr.) indicates. Phil's original concept of how to transmit an image—line by line—is visible.

Television transmission would require many frequencies in order to broadcast pictures as well as sound. One television station would take as much air space as one hundred radio stations. Radio broadcasters were not anxious to see the government assign air space to television.

When the commission held hearings to discuss the matter, it invited Phil to speak. Here was a chance to prove that there was enough space in the air waves for both radio and television. Phil hopped a mail plane to Washington, D.C., an exciting adventure in 1930. After giving an enthusiastic talk, he was back in time to celebrate Christmas with his family.

Soon Phil had another reason to celebrate. On January 15, 1931, his second son, Kenneth, was born. This was a busy, happy time. Phil's work continued to receive a great deal of attention. Even the famous radio company, RCA, took note. In May the company president, David

Sarnoff, came to visit Phil's lab. Although Phil wasn't there, George Everson showed Sarnoff the facilities and answered his questions.

Sarnoff hoped that RCA would be the first to introduce television to the American public, and he must have realized that Farnsworth's work could help him reach that goal. But whatever he really thought at the time, he told Everson that he hadn't seen anything of interest at the Green Street lab. Within months, however, Sarnoff was offering to buy the lab and the Farnsworth patents. Used to getting his own way, he was perfectly willing to buy out the competition. But Farnsworth refused even to consider the offer.

While Sarnoff was touring his lab, Farnsworth had been investigating another opportunity in Philadelphia. Philco Radio Company wanted Farnsworth to sign a licensing deal. He would work for Philco and allow the company to use his patents, but those patents would still belong to him. He would set the course of his work, and Philco would fund his research.

The only drawback was that Phil would have to move to Philadelphia, but at least he could take his whole lab gang with him. They were a close group, almost a second family, and they shared Phil's dedication to electronic television. Phil rented a Pullman train car so all the workers and their families could travel east together. By September everyone had rented houses near each other. On weekdays Phil drove his colleagues to work, and on weekends he took Pem and his sons for long drives in the country.

In Philadelphia, Phil could pick up RCA's broadcasts. One of the early images broadcast by NBC, part of RCA, was that of Felix the cat.

But Phil's happiness didn't last long. In March 1932, fifteen-month-old Kenny died of a streptococcal infection. Phil and Pem never got over Kenny's death, but they forced themselves to keep going. And they both took comfort in their older child. For Christmas Phil gave his son an electric train, just the kind of toy he himself used to admire in the Sears catalog.

Phil spent as much time as he could with Philo Jr., but he still put in long hours at the lab, working to set up an experimental station. This meant he could send programs over air waves to a small number of televisions in different locations. Not far way in Camden, New Jersey, RCA was already doing the same thing with Zworykin's invention, an experimental TV camera called the iconoscope. Phil used his equipment to pick up Zworykin's broadcasts. The pictures were good, he admitted reluctantly, so good that it worried him. The race with RCA was dangerously close. Every time he saw an RCA broadcast, Phil worked harder than ever on his own system.

Phil inspects the workings of one of his early television sets.

Still Waiting for Television

An eager crowd gathered around the Franklin Institute in Philadelphia. It was the summer of 1934, and Phil was ready for a public demonstration. Some of the people in the crowd were tourists who had come to see famous landmarks from America's past. Now Philo Farnsworth was giving them a glimpse of the future—the age of television.

Inside a small auditorium, Phil had set up his largest viewing screen yet. It was thirteen inches wide by twelve inches high, big enough so that all fifty people in the audience had a clear view. Meanwhile Phil supervised the broadcasting from a small studio.

Musicians, dancers, politicians, and dancing bears all had their turn in front of the camera. The studio was crowded, hot, and most of all, bright because the camera needed a great deal of light. Once as Phil watched in dismay, the finish on a musician's cello cracked and splintered under the heat of the glaring lights.

Phil and the lab gang made headlines in 1934 when they spent 10 days broadcasting from the Franklin Institute in Philadelphia. When there was enough sunlight, Phil broadcast on the roof.

Outside Phil set up a small boxing ring and offered passing boys free admission to the show if they would climb inside and ham it up for the camera. Phil was creative and inspired with a camera in his hands. One night, he turned the camera toward a bright, beautiful full moon. The audience thought it was much more exciting to see the moon on television than in the sky. News reporters were impressed too. "First recorded use of television in astronomy," read a headline in the next day's paper.

Phil televised everything from the mayor's opening speech to a tennis demonstration on the roof of the institute. When he finally closed the exhibit after ten days, people all over Philadelphia were wondering when they would have television in their homes.

Even before his success at the Franklin Institute, word of Phil's progress had spread. John Logie Baird asked

Phil to come to England to talk about electronic television. By this time, Phil had left the Philco Company, and the demands of running and financing his own lab left him little free time. But he couldn't pass up a chance like this. He booked passage on the SS *Bremen* and set sail for England with three of his colleagues and crates full of equipment. Baird was so impressed that he decided to take out a license on the Farnsworth patents. This meant that Baird's company would pay Phil in order to use his inventions.

Having a business deal in England was fine, but Phil could hardly wait to use his equipment commercially in his own country. Back in Philadelphia, he continued to work frantically. He designed an experimental station, provided television sets to a small number of homes, and received special government permission to begin broadcasting. Phil had to meet a daily broadcast schedule while he was still improving his equipment. On top of all this, he had to find people talented enough to perform on camera.

Sometimes the pressure was overwhelming. Along with the challenge of keeping his experimental station on the air, Phil had legal problems to face. David Sarnoff and RCA were challenging Phil's claim as the inventor of electronic television. In 1932 the company had begun a legal action called a patent interference. If RCA won, Phil's patents could be set aside, and RCA would be free to use his ideas.

In the suit, RCA lawyers argued that no teenage boy could have thought out all the parts in an electronic television system as Phil claimed he had done back in 1922.

Along with defending his patents, Phil had to maintain a daily schedule of broadcasts at the Farnsworth television studio.

This was a terribly stressful time for Phil. Money that should have gone to his research was used up in legal fees. Hours he could have spent in the lab went to lengthy sessions with his lawyers.

For months, the patent court heard hundreds of hours of testimony from Farnsworth, Zworykin, and others. But the statement that impressed the patent judge most came from Phil's old chemistry teacher, Justin Tolman. Tolman hadn't seen Phil in almost twelve years, but he remembered their talks vividly. He could still recall how Phil planned to use the image dissector and cathode-ray tube to send and receive electronic pictures. Tolman's discussions with Phil had taken place in 1922, a full year before Zworykin had filed his patent application.

When this picture was taken in the 1930s, Phil was beginning to show the strains of constant work and battles over patents.

Finally, the court decided in favor of Philo Farnsworth. A happy celebration broke out in the lab when the legal papers were delivered. But Phil would still have to divide his time between the lab and the lawyers. RCA was appealing the decision.

In the middle of this hectic time, Phil's third son Russell, nicknamed Skee, was born on October 5, 1935. Holding his dark-haired, healthy little boy in his arms, Phil was filled with happiness. One day, however, Skee's pediatrician reminded Phil that not all new parents were as lucky as he and Pem were. Dr. Charles Chapple wanted to save premature babies born too weak and small to survive. He believed that if such babies were placed in closed, germfree cribs, where they could be given oxygen and special tube feedings, many of the infants would live. No one had ever built such a crib before. "If it can be done, you're the guy that can do it," Dr. Chapple told Phil.

The pain of losing Kenny was still very real to Phil. Eager to help other children, he designed a structure called the Isolette and sent it to be tested at Pennsylvania University Hospital. Phil's crib proved to be just what Dr. Chapple needed. Eventually Isolettes were manufactured for use all over the country.

Although inventing the Isolette took up a great deal of time, Phil didn't let up on his television work. In March 1936, RCA had lost its final appeal on the patent decision.

Phil spent long hours working on his inventions, but he also had a strong sense of family. Here he is shown with his son, Skee, in 1935 and with his mother, Serena Farnsworth (below), in 1939.

Now Phil was recognized as the inventor of electronic television. But he had paid a price. Overworked and underweight, Phil was beginning to look much older than his twenty-eight years. Often at meals, his mind was far away, grappling with the problems of the lab.

After much careful thought, Phil decided to form a whole new company. While he waited for the government to set broadcast standards for television, the company would manufacture radios. In the meantime, Phil would take some time off. He had learned the hard way that he couldn't keep up his frantic pace indefinitely. Phil's health was poor, and he was tired and tense. In the spring of 1938, he and Pem took a much-needed vacation to Maine.

Still a farm boy at heart, Phil enjoyed backpacking, fishing, and even wading in a freezing river. But the highlight of his vacation was finding an empty farmhouse. In spite of the neglect and decay, Phil and Pem thought the old home was charming. When Phil scrambled down a hillside out back and discovered a stream, he knew he'd found his perfect getaway. Even before he bought the land, he was already imagining the dam he would build across the stream and the fishpond he would stock.

Now when Phil felt overwhelmed with the pressure of his work, he could dream about his own farm. Later that summer, he returned to Maine to work on his dam. Although he pushed himself hard and was often exhausted, it was a good kind of tired. Phil enjoyed physical labor and was glad to escape from the endless paperwork and financial meetings he faced in Philadelphia. But he was pleased with the way the new company was developing and glad when Farnsworth Television and Radio bought two radio factories in Indiana. These factories could be adapted to make televisions someday.

The FCC still hadn't set guidelines for commercial broadcasting, but Phil and others wanted to be ready to produce television sets when they did. In 1939 RCA introduced television to millions of Americans at the New York World's Fair. Television was a big hit, but RCA couldn't make it practical without using parts of Farnsworth's system. After the World's Fair, RCA agreed to pay Farnsworth royalties for using his patents. Phil could channel this money back into his own research.

By Christmas the Farnsworths had moved to Fort Wayne, Indiana, where the research department of Phil's new company was located. A few months before, war had broken out in Europe. Phil suspected that the fighting would delay the development of television in the United States. For years he had given all his time and talent to television. He had waited and waited for the government to set broadcast standards. But he found it hard to wait any longer. Gradually Phil began to lose interest in his research—and even in the people around him. Pem and others worried about Phil's health. Finally Phil returned to his farm in Maine to recover from a nervous breakdown.

Phil was right about the war affecting television. On April 1, 1941, the United States government issued emergency instructions declaring that commercial radio and television set production should stop at once. What happened next must have been especially frustrating to Phil.

The 1939 World's Fair in New York presented crowds with many wonders and visions of the future. Few were as exciting as the display of a television created by Farnsworth's rival, RCA.

The FCC finally adopted standards for commercial television. Phil had wanted this to happen for years. Now it was too late. All available resources had to be conserved in case the United States became involved in the war.

Since Phil couldn't start manufacturing television sets, he decided not to return to his factories in Fort Wayne. He could build a lab right onto his farmhouse and start working on other inventions. The one thing he tried not to think about was television. As far as he was concerned, his work with television was through.

New Goals

Frail and thin, Phil suffered many health problems during the war. Sometimes he was so ill he could spend only an hour a day in his lab. But he never forgot he was an inventor, and he had other projects to interest him.

Still fascinated by vacuum tubes, he realized they had many uses besides television. When the United States entered the war, Phil modified the image dissector into an instrument called a sniperscope which allowed soldiers to see in the dark. Phil's factories in Indiana made sniperscopes, radios, and radar sets for military airplanes. The government wanted Phil's help in another way also. Officials asked him to join the Manhattan Project, a top secret research effort to develop an atomic bomb. But for once Phil turned down a research project. He didn't want to help make such a destructive weapon.

During World War II, Phil continued to experiment and to invent, but he tried to keep his mind off his most famous invention—television.

Instead he helped the war effort by buying a forest near his home in Maine and making wooden crates for government shipments overseas. When World War II ended with the explosion of atomic bombs at Hiroshima and Nagasaki, Phil began thinking about peaceful uses for atomic reactions.

But Phil had other issues to deal with too. Although he loved Maine, his company's officials urged him to return to Fort Wayne after the war. Farnsworth Television was having financial problems and needed Phil's leadership on a daily basis. Then in October 1947, a terrible fire swept through rural Maine. For three days, the flames grew in intensity despite the frantic efforts of firefighters. Friends came to help Phil and Pem move their belongings. Soon the fire's rapid approach forced everyone to evacuate the area. The family jumped into the car and drove away. Stopping behind Phil's dam, they watched, heartbroken, as flames destroyed their home and Phil's lab and library. Sparks rained down on the car when they drove to safety.

Shocked by the fire and saddened by the recent death of his brother Carl, Phil fell into a deep depression. But he slowly came to terms with his losses and began to think about the future—and about television. After the war, the FCC lifted the ban on manufacturing television sets. By the middle of 1946, it had begun licensing stations. About seven thousand Americans owned television sets, but Phil knew this was just the beginning. Although he'd said he was through with television, he became excited in spite of himself. He felt he owed it to his investors to make Farnsworth Television a success.

The year 1949 was a busy one. In May Philo Jr. was married. In June Phil, Pem, and Skee moved to Fort Wayne. There Phil would manufacture television sets, continue research, and enter the field of broadcasting. In September, Pem gave birth to a fourth boy named Kent.

Early Farnsworth televisions were housed in large wooden cabinets but still had very small screens by modern standards.

At forty-three, Phil was delighted to be a father again. But his professional life wasn't as happy as his personal life. Farnsworth Television just didn't have the funds to compete with large companies like RCA. Phil's earliest patents had begun to expire in 1947, so he'd lost the advantage he would have had if commercial television had begun sooner. Not long after the family moved, he reluctantly sold the company to International Telephone and Telegraph, or ITT.

As the months passed, Phil realized that ITT wasn't interested in making televisions or in broadcasting. Now his hopes for working in television were truly over. It hurt to let go of his ambitions a second time. But Phil was strengthened by the support of his family and the joy of seeing his baby son grow. He brought his drive and creativity to problems even more challenging than television.

For many years Phil investigated nuclear fusion—trying to fuse, or join, atoms together. (This is the opposite of what happens in an atomic bomb when atoms are split apart.) Phil believed that fusion would release enormous amounts of energy that could be used to power cities. With a device he invented called a Fusor, Phil sometimes obtained promising results. But he couldn't duplicate them or make other people understand all his theories.

Phil never regretted buying a violin instead of a bicycle from the Sears catalog. Throughout his life, he enjoyed playing the violin and picking out tunes on the piano.

The work Phil did on military contracts for the government proved more practical than his fusion experiments. Phil helped develop a radar system that could spot and destroy an approaching missile. He invented a tube called the Iatron that stored information and made it easier for air traffic controllers to monitor planes coming and going in airports.

Meanwhile, commercial television was growing into a big business. By 1950 there were seven million televisions in the United States. Companies couldn't build sets fast enough. Instead of a few hours a day, some stations were broadcasting from morning until midnight. Even though Phil wasn't part of the growing industry, some people remembered that it all began with him.

In 1950 he flew to San Francisco to help dedicate a TV cable link between that city and Los Angeles. Now shows broadcast in one city could be seen in the other. Three years later, Phil went to Idaho for the first time since his boyhood. The state's first television station was ready to begin broadcasting, and Phil played an important part in the opening ceremonies.

Television pictures still weren't as sharp and well-defined as they are nowadays. In the Fort Wayne area where Phil lived, television reception was so poor that he didn't even own a working set. Then his youngest son learned that all the other first graders had televisions in their homes. Something would have to change, Kent told his father. Phil agreed and bought a television for his son.

Philo Farnsworth wasn't exactly a household name. He had never achieved the fame of his boyhood heroes

Alexander Graham Bell and Thomas Edison. But in 1957 when he appeared on the television show *I've Got a Secret,* host Garry Moore introduced him as "Mr. X." Panelists had to guess each contestant's secret, and Moore felt sure Phil's name would give his secret away. While Phil whispered in Garry Moore's ear, the words flashed on television sets all across the country: "I invented electronic television in 1922 at the age of fourteen."

Then the camera showed Phil's face again. Viewers saw a very thin man in his early fifties with a high, lined forehead and a quiet smile. His eyes twinkled behind wire-rimmed glasses. After so many years of struggling to make television work, it must have been fun to be on the opposite end of the camera.

In 1967 Phil and Pem returned to Utah. A television station was making a documentary on Phil's life. More than forty years had passed since they'd left the state as newlyweds, but it still seemed so much like home that they decided to move back permanently. Phil bought a house, set up a new research organization, and became an elder in the Mormon Church.

By this time, almost every household in the United States boasted at least one television set. Sometimes Phil wondered if this was really a good thing. He had imagined that television would become a great educational resource. Some of the programs in the 1950s and 1960s seemed downright ridiculous to him. He even told Pem he was sorry he had anything to do with TV. But the day he watched men walk on the moon in 1969, he decided that the good outweighed the bad after all.

Not long after they met, Phil told Pem, "Pem, I think we were meant for each other." They remained partners in work and in life until Phil's death. Here they review papers in the breakfast room of their Utah home in 1969.

Phil believed that even more amazing advances lay in the future, and he wanted to be part of them. But on March 11, 1971, he died of heart failure following a bout of pneumonia. Although he hadn't achieved all his goals, the theories he'd developed when he was only fourteen had changed the lives of people all over the world. "The difficult we do at once; the impossible takes a little longer," he liked to remind people.

Philo Farnsworth proved his favorite saying. He did indeed accomplish the impossible.

Afterword

In 1985 the children at Ridgecrest Elementary School in Salt Lake City, Utah, launched a campaign that would take them all the way to Washington, D.C. They had learned that every state is allowed to put two statues in the United States Capitol, but Utah had only one. It was time for a second statue, they decided.

First the children pored over the history books, looking for someone worthy of the honor. Then they sent surveys to adults and to children at other schools. They interviewed people in shopping malls to see who Utah residents wanted in the Capitol building. Soon they realized that Philo Farnsworth was the people's choice for Utah's second statue.

Representative Donald R. LeBaron helped the children by introducing a bill into the Utah legislature. The bill called for a statue of Philo Taylor Farnsworth to be commissioned for the Capitol. In 1987 both houses of the state government passed the bill, and Governor Norman Bangerter signed it into law. James Avati was chosen to sculpt the work, and children all over Utah held fundraisers to pay part of the costs.

This model of Utah's second statue in the Capitol Rotunda shows Philo T. Farnsworth thinking, as usual, about an invention.

On May 2, 1990, a crowd of excited people filled the Capitol building's Statuary Hall. Most of the people—especially the children—had worked hard for this moment. After several speeches, the statue was unveiled. The children saw a young, serious Philo holding an early television camera tube. He seemed to be deep in thought, as if thinking up ways he could improve his invention.

"If Phil were here," Pem Farnsworth declared, "he would say, 'Follow your dreams, because nothing is impossible.'"

Notes

Page 18

Asael Tall still recalls his father's annoyance at Philo's repeated experiments with the generator. Once Mr. Tall said in exasperation that he would find Philo a generator of his own if only he would leave the one that powered the farm alone. After Philo learned to repair the generator himself, it continued to break down frequently. Occasionally his parents wondered if he broke it on purpose just for the fun of fixing it.

Page 40

Philo Farnsworth wasn't the first person to think of electronic television. In 1908 an English electrical engineer named A. Swinton Campbell planned a way to transmit and receive television pictures entirely through electronic means. He never tried to build the system because he felt the technology didn't exist yet to make it practical. However, other scientists were already experimenting with electronics. In Germany Max Dieckmann and in Russia Boris Rosing tried using cathode-ray tubes to receive television pictures. But they didn't use electronic means to transmit these pictures. In the United States, Gilbert Sellars, another television pioneer, also used a combination of electronics and mechanical parts. Of all these inventors, only Farnsworth created a totally electronic system that worked.

Page 61

The more lines in a television picture, the sharper that picture is. It takes 525 lines to make up a single picture on a modern television. Every second 30 pictures are received on the television screen.

In the 1940s, Phil often took time off and headed to Maine. Here Cliff *(left)* and Phil go backpacking.

Page 63

Although both the image dissector and the iconoscope were early television cameras, they worked differently. Zworykin's iconoscope contained thousands of tiny photoelectric cells which became electrically charged when struck by light. These charges were the electrical equivalent of the picture to be televised. A beam of electrons scanned the plate with the photoelectric cells. It collected the charges into a straight line which could be amplified (strengthened) and passed to the transmitter. Because the iconoscope was able to store light, it could operate under dimmer conditions than the image dissector and get a brighter picture.

Page 68

On August 24, 1934, the *Philadelphia Evening Public Ledger* made some predictions that seemed fantastic at the time but would soon come true: "While [television's] ultimate potentialities can only be estimated now, it is thought that it will bring nearer the day when a person may sit in his home and see a movie or enjoy a sports contest. The system is devised so that its receiving set could easily be placed in a convenient sized cabinet suitable for any home."

Page 82
Phil considered his fusion experiments the most important work he had ever done. He predicted that someday humans would be able to control climate, change the desert into farmland, and travel to the stars with the power obtained from fusion.

Page 83
In his lifetime, Philo Farnsworth received approximately 150 United States patents, many related to television. He also had over one hundred foreign patents.

Bibliography

Books:

Abramson, Albert. *The History of Television, 1880–1941.* Jefferson, NC: McFarland & Company, Inc., Publishers, 1987.

Barnouw, Erik. *Tube of Plenty: The Evolution of American Television.* 2d rev. ed. New York: Oxford University Press, 1990.

Compton's Encyclopedia. New York: Compton's New Media, Inc., and Compton's Learning Company, 1995.

Everson, George. *The Story of Television: The Life of Philo T. Farnsworth.* New York: W. W. Norton & Company, Inc., 1949.

Farnsworth, Mrs. Elma G. "Pem." *Distant Vision: Romance and Discovery on an Invisible Frontier.* Salt Lake City, UT: PemberlyKent Publishers, Inc., undated.

Flatow, Ira. *They All Laughed . . . From Light Bulbs to Lasers: The Fascinating Stories Behind the Great Inventions That Have Changed Our Lives.* New York: HarperCollins Publishers, 1992.

Goldstein, Norm. *Associated Press History of Television.* New York: Portland House, 1991.

Kisseloff, Jeff. *The Box: An Oral History of Television, 1920–1961.* New York: Viking, 1995.

McGraw-Hill Encyclopedia of Science and Technology. Vol. 18. 7th ed. New York: McGraw-Hill, Inc., 1992.

*Morgan, Jane. *Electronics in the West: The First Fifty Years.* Palo Alto, CA: National Press Books, 1967.

Ritchie, Michael. *Please Stand By: A Prehistory of Television.* Woodstock, NY: The Overlook Press, 1994.

Waldrop, Frank C., and Joseph Borkin. *Television: A Struggle for Power.* 1938. Reprint, New York: Arno Press and The New York Times, 1971.

A Farnsworth television camera

Periodicals and Documents:

Abramson, Albert. "Pioneers of Television—Philo Taylor Farnsworth." *SMPTE Journal* (November 1992).

*Boring, Mel. "The New Wonder Window." *Cobblestone* (October 1989).

Carskadon, T. R. "Phil, the Inventor." *Collier's* (October 3, 1936).

Hofner, Stephen F. "Philo Farnsworth: Television's Pioneer." *Journal of Broadcasting* (Spring 1979).

Lovece, Frank. "Zworykin v. Farnsworth Part I." *Video* (August 1985).

Lovece, Frank. "Zworykin v. Farnsworth Part II." *Video* (September 1985).

Minton, James. "Tom Swift in San Francisco: Philo T. Farnsworth and His Electric Television." *San Francisco Monthly* (November 1972).

Noall, Claire. "From Utah Farm Boy to Inventor of Television Fascinating Story." *Deseret News* (November 14, 1948).

*Olson, Jeanne Field. "Philo Farnsworth: Forgotten Inventor." *Cobblestone* (October 1989).

Ormond, Clyde. "'Mr. Television' Visited Here with Old School-mates." *The Rigby Star* (July 16, 1953).

"Philo T. Farnsworth Dies at 64, Known as Father of Television." *Deseret News* (March 12, 1971).

Philo T. Farnsworth Papers. University of Utah Marriott Library, Salt Lake City, UT.

Record of the 101st Congress, 2d Session. House Document 101–188. Acceptance and Dedication of the Statue of Philo T. Farnsworth Presented by the State of Utah. Proceedings in the Rotunda of the United States Capitol, Washington, D.C. May 2, 1990.

Roop, Thomas. "The Real Father of Television." *Arizona Republic* (1984). Reprint, *Deseret News Magazine* (October 21, 1989).

"Television Set Called Ephochal." *Philadelphia Evening Public Ledger* (August 24, 1934).

Video:

I've Got a Secret. CBS. Segment in which Philo Farnsworth appeared. 1957.

Interviews with Author:

Dr. Asael Tall, childhood friend of Philo Farnsworth, Rigby, ID, July and December 1994.

*An asterisk denotes material for younger readers.
All quotations in this book are taken from the sources above.

Index

Phil shows scientist Dr. Rolf Mueller around the lab.

Acknowledgments

I would like especially to thank Mrs. Philo Farnsworth for generously sharing her time, memories, and videotaped news coverage of her husband's achievements.

Special thanks also go to Dr. Priscilla Cushman of the University of Minnesota's Department of Physics for her valuable help on the scientific portions of this book and to my editor Gwenyth Swain for her insights and suggestions.

I would also like to thank Dr. Asael Tall, Dr. Bruce Barnson, Seymour Stein, Dot Dabell, Gary Hainsworth, Aston Broulim, and Mrs. Clyde Ormond for their help. In addition, I am indebted to the Salt Lake City Public Library, the Idaho Falls Library, the Marriott Library of the University of Utah, and the Franklin Institute Science Museum of Philadelphia for providing materials.

Excerpts from the following works appear by permission on the pages noted: *Distant Vision: Romance and Discovery on an Invisible Frontier* by Mrs. Elma G. "Pem" Farnsworth (Salt Lake City, UT: PemberlyKent Publishers, Inc., undated), pages 5, 24, 28, 42, 43, 48, 49, 55, 58, 59, 63, 70, 74, 84, and 85; Record of the 101st Congress, 2d Session, House Document 101–188, pages 29 and 85; *The Story of Television: The Life of Philo T. Farnsworth* by George Everson (New York: W. W. Norton & Company, Inc., 1949), pages 40, 41, and 46; "From Utah Farm Boy to Inventor of Television Fascinating Story" by Claire Noall, *Deseret News* (November 14, 1948), pages 23 and 52.

Illustrations are reproduced through the courtesy of: Special Collections, University of Utah Library, Salt Lake City, UT, front cover (photograph), pp. 2, 19, 34, 49, 57, 62, 65, 70, 72, 73, 74 (both), 79, 81, 82, 85, 87, 88, 92, 95; U.S. Patent Office, front cover (background diagram); UPI/Bettmann Newsphotos, back cover, pp. 55, 58, 63, 68; The Bettmann Archive, pp. 6, 21, 41; Utah State Historical Society, all rights reserved, used with permission, pp. 9, 13, 15, 16; Mrs. Elma G. "Pem" Farnsworth, pp. 11, 32, 39, 42, 50, 52; Library of Congress, pp. 22, 77; U.S. Department of the Interior, p. 26; Rigby Historical Society, pp. 29, 31; Archive Photos, pp. 30, 67; Laura Westlund, p. 45.